50 Pasta Perfect: Italian Classics and Beyond Recipes

By: Kelly Johnson

Table of Contents

- Spaghetti Carbonara
- Lasagna Bolognese
- Fettuccine Alfredo
- Penne Arrabbiata
- Rigatoni alla Norma
- Pappardelle with Porcini Mushrooms
- Tagliatelle with Truffle Cream Sauce
- Tortellini in Brodo
- Gnocchi with Sage Butter
- Orecchiette with Broccoli Rabe
- Spaghetti Aglio e Olio
- Pesto Genovese with Trofie
- Baked Ziti
- Pasta Primavera
- Cacio e Pepe
- Cannelloni with Spinach and Ricotta
- Fettuccine with Shrimp and Lemon
- Spaghetti Puttanesca
- Pappardelle with Wild Boar Ragù
- Fusilli with Pesto Rosso
- Spaghetti with Clams (Spaghetti alle Vongole)
- Lasagna Verde with Pesto
- Pasta e Fagioli
- Macaroni and Cheese (Italian Style)
- Ravioli with Butter and Parmesan
- Fregola Sarda with Lobster
- Tortelloni with Butternut Squash and Brown Butter
- Penne alla Vodka
- Farfalle with Smoked Salmon and Cream
- Spaghetti with Meatballs
- Penne with Sausage and Peppers
- Capellini with Cherry Tomatoes and Basil
- Gnocchi with Gorgonzola and Walnuts
- Cavatelli with Sausage and Broccoli
- Lasagna with Ricotta and Spinach

- Pici with Garlic and Olive Oil
- Strozzapreti with Sausage and Mushrooms
- Fettuccine with Asparagus and Parmesan
- Linguine with Lobster
- Pasta al Pomodoro
- Spaghetti with Zucchini and Mint
- Orecchiette with Sausage and Kale
- Mafaldini with Shrimp and Saffron
- Lasagna Caprese
- Pasta alla Caprese
- Penne with Roasted Vegetables
- Ravioli with Sweet Potato and Sage
- Fettuccine with Spicy Sausage
- Rigatoni with Eggplant and Ricotta
- Pappardelle with Duck Ragù

Spaghetti Carbonara

Ingredients:

- 400g spaghetti
- 150g pancetta or guanciale, diced
- 3 large eggs
- 1 cup Pecorino Romano cheese, grated
- 1/2 cup Parmigiano Reggiano, grated
- 2 garlic cloves, peeled
- Freshly ground black pepper
- Salt for pasta water

Directions:

1. Bring a large pot of salted water to a boil and cook the spaghetti according to package instructions. Reserve 1 cup of pasta water before draining.
2. While the pasta is cooking, heat a pan over medium heat. Add the pancetta or guanciale and cook until crispy, about 5 minutes. Add the garlic cloves and cook for 1-2 minutes until fragrant. Remove the garlic.
3. In a mixing bowl, whisk the eggs, Pecorino Romano, Parmigiano Reggiano, and a good amount of black pepper.
4. Once the pasta is cooked and drained, add it to the pan with the pancetta. Toss to coat.
5. Quickly pour the egg and cheese mixture over the pasta, tossing constantly to create a creamy sauce. Add reserved pasta water a little at a time to reach your desired sauce consistency.
6. Serve immediately, garnished with more black pepper and grated cheese.

Lasagna Bolognese

Ingredients:

- 12 lasagna noodles (pre-cooked or fresh)
- 2 tbsp olive oil
- 1 onion, chopped
- 2 garlic cloves, minced
- 1 lb ground beef
- 1 lb ground pork
- 1 carrot, chopped
- 1 celery stalk, chopped
- 1 can (14 oz) crushed tomatoes
- 1/2 cup red wine
- 1 cup whole milk
- 1/2 tsp nutmeg
- Salt and pepper to taste
- 3 cups ricotta cheese
- 2 cups mozzarella cheese, shredded
- 1/2 cup Parmigiano Reggiano, grated

Directions:

1. Preheat the oven to 375°F (190°C).
2. In a large pot, heat olive oil over medium heat. Add the onion, garlic, carrot, and celery, cooking until softened.
3. Add the ground beef and pork, cooking until browned. Stir in the crushed tomatoes, red wine, milk, nutmeg, salt, and pepper. Simmer for 45 minutes.
4. In a bowl, combine the ricotta, mozzarella, and Parmigiano Reggiano. Season with a pinch of salt.
5. Cook the lasagna noodles according to the package instructions.
6. In a large baking dish, spread a thin layer of the Bolognese sauce, then layer with lasagna noodles, ricotta mixture, and more sauce. Repeat the layers until the dish is filled. Finish with a layer of sauce and mozzarella.
7. Cover with foil and bake for 30 minutes. Remove the foil and bake for another 10 minutes to brown the top.
8. Let the lasagna rest for 10 minutes before serving.

Fettuccine Alfredo

Ingredients:

- 400g fettuccine
- 1 cup heavy cream
- 1/2 cup butter
- 1 cup Parmigiano Reggiano, grated
- 1/2 cup Pecorino Romano, grated
- Salt and pepper to taste

Directions:

1. Cook the fettuccine in a large pot of salted boiling water until al dente. Drain, reserving some pasta water.
2. In a large pan, melt the butter over medium heat. Add the heavy cream and cook, stirring occasionally, until heated through.
3. Stir in the grated Parmigiano Reggiano and Pecorino Romano. Continue to cook, stirring, until the cheese is melted and the sauce thickens.
4. Add the cooked fettuccine to the pan and toss to coat. If the sauce is too thick, add some reserved pasta water to achieve the desired consistency.
5. Season with salt and pepper to taste. Serve immediately.

Penne Arrabbiata

Ingredients:

- 400g penne pasta
- 2 tbsp olive oil
- 4 garlic cloves, thinly sliced
- 1/2 tsp red pepper flakes
- 1 can (14 oz) crushed tomatoes
- 1/2 cup fresh basil, chopped
- Salt and pepper to taste
- Grated Parmigiano Reggiano for serving

Directions:

1. Cook the penne pasta in salted boiling water according to package instructions. Drain, reserving some pasta water.
2. In a large pan, heat olive oil over medium heat. Add the garlic and red pepper flakes, cooking until fragrant but not browned, about 1-2 minutes.
3. Stir in the crushed tomatoes and simmer for 10 minutes. Season with salt and pepper.
4. Add the cooked penne to the sauce, tossing to coat. If the sauce is too thick, add some reserved pasta water.
5. Stir in the chopped basil and serve with grated Parmigiano Reggiano.

Rigatoni alla Norma

Ingredients:

- 400g rigatoni pasta
- 2 tbsp olive oil
- 1 eggplant, cut into cubes
- 2 garlic cloves, minced
- 1 can (14 oz) crushed tomatoes
- 1/4 cup fresh basil, chopped
- 1 cup ricotta salata, grated
- Salt and pepper to taste

Directions:

1. Cook the rigatoni in salted boiling water according to package instructions. Drain, reserving some pasta water.
2. In a large pan, heat olive oil over medium heat. Add the eggplant and cook until golden and tender, about 8-10 minutes. Remove the eggplant from the pan and set aside.
3. In the same pan, add the garlic and cook for 1 minute. Stir in the crushed tomatoes and simmer for 10 minutes. Season with salt and pepper.
4. Add the cooked rigatoni and eggplant to the sauce, tossing to coat. If the sauce is too thick, add some reserved pasta water.
5. Stir in the chopped basil and serve with grated ricotta salata.

Pappardelle with Porcini Mushrooms

Ingredients:

- 400g pappardelle pasta
- 2 tbsp olive oil
- 1/2 lb porcini mushrooms, sliced (or substitute with other wild mushrooms)
- 2 garlic cloves, minced
- 1/4 cup white wine
- 1/2 cup heavy cream
- 1/4 cup fresh parsley, chopped
- Salt and pepper to taste
- Grated Parmigiano Reggiano for serving

Directions:

1. Cook the pappardelle in salted boiling water according to package instructions. Drain, reserving some pasta water.
2. In a large pan, heat olive oil over medium heat. Add the mushrooms and cook until tender and browned, about 8-10 minutes.
3. Stir in the garlic and cook for 1 minute. Add the white wine and cook for 2 minutes to reduce.
4. Pour in the heavy cream and simmer for 5 minutes, allowing the sauce to thicken. Season with salt and pepper.
5. Add the cooked pappardelle to the sauce, tossing to coat. If the sauce is too thick, add some reserved pasta water.
6. Stir in the fresh parsley and serve with grated Parmigiano Reggiano.

Tagliatelle with Truffle Cream Sauce

Ingredients:

- 400g tagliatelle pasta
- 2 tbsp olive oil
- 1/2 cup heavy cream
- 2 tbsp butter
- 1/4 cup truffle oil
- 1/4 cup Parmigiano Reggiano, grated
- Salt and pepper to taste
- Fresh parsley for garnish

Directions:

1. Cook the tagliatelle in salted boiling water according to package instructions. Drain, reserving some pasta water.
2. In a large pan, melt the butter and heat the olive oil over medium heat.
3. Stir in the heavy cream and simmer for 2-3 minutes until the sauce thickens slightly.
4. Add the truffle oil and stir to combine. Season with salt and pepper.
5. Add the cooked tagliatelle to the pan, tossing to coat. If the sauce is too thick, add some reserved pasta water.
6. Stir in the grated Parmigiano Reggiano and garnish with fresh parsley.

Tortellini in Brodo

Ingredients:

- 400g fresh tortellini (cheese or meat-filled)
- 4 cups chicken or vegetable broth
- 1 carrot, chopped
- 1 celery stalk, chopped
- 1 onion, peeled and halved
- 2 garlic cloves, smashed
- Fresh parsley for garnish
- Salt and pepper to taste

Directions:

1. In a large pot, bring the broth to a boil. Add the carrot, celery, onion, and garlic. Simmer for 30 minutes to allow the flavors to develop.
2. Strain the broth, discarding the vegetables and aromatics. Return the broth to the pot.
3. Bring the broth to a boil again, and add the fresh tortellini. Cook according to package instructions, about 3-5 minutes.
4. Season with salt and pepper to taste.
5. Serve hot, garnished with fresh parsley.

Gnocchi with Sage Butter

Ingredients:

- 500g potato gnocchi (store-bought or homemade)
- 4 tbsp unsalted butter
- 12 fresh sage leaves
- Salt and pepper to taste
- Grated Parmigiano Reggiano for serving

Directions:

1. Cook the gnocchi in salted boiling water according to package instructions. Once they float to the top, remove them and set aside.
2. In a large pan, melt the butter over medium heat. Add the sage leaves and cook for 2-3 minutes, allowing the butter to brown slightly.
3. Add the cooked gnocchi to the pan and toss gently to coat in the sage butter.
4. Season with salt and pepper to taste. Serve immediately with grated Parmigiano Reggiano.

Orecchiette with Broccoli Rabe

Ingredients:

- 400g orecchiette pasta
- 1 bunch broccoli rabe, trimmed and chopped
- 3 tbsp olive oil
- 4 garlic cloves, minced
- 1/2 tsp red pepper flakes
- Salt and pepper to taste
- Grated Pecorino Romano for serving

Directions:

1. Cook the orecchiette in salted boiling water according to package instructions. Reserve some pasta water before draining.
2. In a large pan, heat olive oil over medium heat. Add the garlic and red pepper flakes, cooking until fragrant, about 1 minute.
3. Add the chopped broccoli rabe and cook for 4-5 minutes until tender. Season with salt and pepper.
4. Add the cooked orecchiette to the pan, tossing to combine. Add some reserved pasta water if the sauce needs loosening.
5. Serve with grated Pecorino Romano.

Spaghetti Aglio e Olio

Ingredients:

- 400g spaghetti
- 6 garlic cloves, thinly sliced
- 1/4 cup olive oil
- 1/2 tsp red pepper flakes
- Fresh parsley, chopped
- Salt and pepper to taste
- Grated Parmigiano Reggiano for serving

Directions:

1. Cook the spaghetti in salted boiling water according to package instructions. Reserve some pasta water before draining.
2. In a large pan, heat olive oil over medium heat. Add the garlic and red pepper flakes, cooking until the garlic is golden and fragrant, about 2 minutes.
3. Add the cooked spaghetti to the pan, tossing to coat in the garlic oil. Add some reserved pasta water to help create a sauce.
4. Season with salt and pepper and garnish with fresh parsley. Serve with grated Parmigiano Reggiano.

Pesto Genovese with Trofie

Ingredients:

- 400g trofie pasta
- 1 cup fresh basil leaves
- 1/4 cup pine nuts
- 2 garlic cloves
- 1/2 cup extra virgin olive oil
- 1/2 cup Parmigiano Reggiano, grated
- Salt to taste

Directions:

1. Cook the trofie pasta in salted boiling water according to package instructions. Reserve some pasta water before draining.
2. In a food processor, combine the basil, pine nuts, garlic, olive oil, and Parmigiano Reggiano. Blend until smooth, adding salt to taste.
3. Toss the cooked trofie with the pesto sauce, adding reserved pasta water as needed to thin the sauce.
4. Serve with additional grated Parmigiano Reggiano.

Baked Ziti

Ingredients:

- 400g ziti pasta
- 1 jar (24 oz) marinara sauce
- 2 cups ricotta cheese
- 2 cups mozzarella cheese, shredded
- 1/2 cup Parmigiano Reggiano, grated
- Fresh basil for garnish
- Salt and pepper to taste

Directions:

1. Preheat the oven to 375°F (190°C).
2. Cook the ziti pasta in salted boiling water according to package instructions. Drain and set aside.
3. In a mixing bowl, combine the ricotta cheese, half of the mozzarella, and Parmigiano Reggiano. Season with salt and pepper.
4. In a large baking dish, spread a thin layer of marinara sauce. Add a layer of cooked ziti, then top with ricotta mixture and more marinara sauce. Repeat the layers, finishing with mozzarella on top.
5. Cover with foil and bake for 25 minutes. Remove the foil and bake for an additional 10 minutes to brown the top.
6. Garnish with fresh basil before serving.

Pasta Primavera

Ingredients:

- 400g penne or fusilli pasta
- 2 tbsp olive oil
- 1 zucchini, sliced
- 1 bell pepper, sliced
- 1 carrot, julienned
- 1 cup cherry tomatoes, halved
- 1/2 cup fresh basil, chopped
- 1/2 cup grated Parmigiano Reggiano
- Salt and pepper to taste

Directions:

1. Cook the pasta in salted boiling water according to package instructions. Reserve some pasta water before draining.
2. In a large pan, heat olive oil over medium heat. Add the zucchini, bell pepper, and carrot, and cook for 5-7 minutes until tender.
3. Stir in the cherry tomatoes and cook for another 2 minutes.
4. Add the cooked pasta to the pan and toss to combine, adding reserved pasta water if needed.
5. Season with salt and pepper, and garnish with fresh basil and grated Parmigiano Reggiano. Serve immediately.

Cacio e Pepe

Ingredients:

- 400g spaghetti
- 1/2 cup Pecorino Romano cheese, grated
- 1/4 cup Parmigiano Reggiano, grated
- 1 tsp black pepper, freshly cracked
- Salt for pasta water

Directions:

1. Cook the spaghetti in salted boiling water according to package instructions. Reserve some pasta water before draining.
2. In a large pan, toast the black pepper over medium heat for 1 minute to release its flavor.
3. Add the cooked pasta to the pan, tossing to coat in the toasted pepper.
4. Gradually add the Pecorino Romano and Parmigiano Reggiano, stirring constantly, and add reserved pasta water a little at a time to create a creamy sauce.
5. Serve immediately, garnished with more cheese and pepper.

Cannelloni with Spinach and Ricotta

Ingredients:

- 12 cannelloni tubes
- 1 lb spinach, cooked and chopped
- 2 cups ricotta cheese
- 1/2 cup Parmigiano Reggiano, grated
- 1 egg
- 1 jar (24 oz) marinara sauce
- Salt and pepper to taste

Directions:

1. Preheat the oven to 375°F (190°C).
2. Cook the cannelloni tubes in salted boiling water until al dente. Drain and set aside.
3. In a mixing bowl, combine the cooked spinach, ricotta cheese, Parmigiano Reggiano, and egg. Season with salt and pepper.
4. Stuff the cooked cannelloni with the spinach and ricotta mixture.
5. Spread a thin layer of marinara sauce in the bottom of a baking dish. Arrange the stuffed cannelloni in the dish and cover with more marinara sauce.
6. Cover with foil and bake for 30 minutes. Remove the foil and bake for an additional 10 minutes.
7. Serve hot, garnished with more grated Parmigiano Reggiano.

Fettuccine with Shrimp and Lemon

Ingredients:

- 400g fettuccine pasta
- 1 lb shrimp, peeled and deveined
- 2 tbsp olive oil
- 2 garlic cloves, minced
- 1 lemon, zested and juiced
- 1/2 cup heavy cream
- 1/2 cup Parmesan cheese, grated
- Salt and pepper to taste
- Fresh parsley for garnish

Directions:

1. Cook the fettuccine in salted boiling water according to package instructions. Drain, reserving some pasta water.
2. In a large pan, heat olive oil over medium heat. Add the shrimp and cook for 2-3 minutes on each side until pink and cooked through. Remove the shrimp and set aside.
3. In the same pan, add the garlic and cook for 1 minute. Add the lemon zest and juice, and stir in the heavy cream.
4. Bring the sauce to a simmer and cook for 2-3 minutes until slightly thickened.
5. Add the cooked fettuccine and shrimp to the pan, tossing to coat. Add reserved pasta water as needed to adjust the sauce consistency.
6. Stir in the grated Parmesan and season with salt and pepper. Garnish with fresh parsley and serve.

Spaghetti Puttanesca

Ingredients:

- 400g spaghetti
- 3 tbsp olive oil
- 4 garlic cloves, minced
- 1 can (400g) diced tomatoes
- 1/2 cup Kalamata olives, pitted and chopped
- 2 tbsp capers
- 4 anchovy fillets, chopped
- 1/2 tsp red pepper flakes
- Salt and pepper to taste
- Fresh parsley, chopped
- Grated Parmigiano Reggiano for serving

Directions:

1. Cook the spaghetti in salted boiling water according to package instructions. Reserve some pasta water before draining.
2. In a large pan, heat the olive oil over medium heat. Add the garlic and cook for 1 minute, then add the anchovies and red pepper flakes, cooking until the anchovies dissolve.
3. Add the diced tomatoes, olives, and capers, and simmer for 10 minutes, allowing the sauce to thicken.
4. Add the cooked spaghetti to the sauce, tossing to combine. Add reserved pasta water to adjust the sauce consistency.
5. Season with salt and pepper, then garnish with fresh parsley and serve with grated Parmigiano Reggiano.

Pappardelle with Wild Boar Ragù

Ingredients:

- 400g pappardelle pasta
- 500g wild boar meat, cubed
- 2 tbsp olive oil
- 1 onion, chopped
- 2 garlic cloves, minced
- 1 carrot, chopped
- 1 celery stalk, chopped
- 1/2 cup red wine
- 1 can (400g) diced tomatoes
- 1 tbsp tomato paste
- 1 tsp dried rosemary
- Salt and pepper to taste
- Fresh parsley, chopped
- Grated Pecorino Romano for serving

Directions:

1. Cook the pappardelle in salted boiling water according to package instructions. Reserve some pasta water before draining.
2. In a large pot, heat olive oil over medium heat. Add the wild boar meat and brown on all sides. Remove and set aside.
3. In the same pot, sauté onion, garlic, carrot, and celery until softened.
4. Add the wine and cook for 2 minutes, scraping any browned bits from the bottom of the pot.
5. Stir in the diced tomatoes, tomato paste, rosemary, and reserved wild boar. Simmer for 1.5 to 2 hours, until the ragù thickens and the meat is tender.
6. Toss the cooked pappardelle with the ragù and add reserved pasta water as needed to adjust the sauce.
7. Serve with fresh parsley and grated Pecorino Romano.

Fusilli with Pesto Rosso

Ingredients:

- 400g fusilli pasta
- 1/2 cup sun-dried tomatoes
- 1/4 cup almonds or pine nuts
- 1 garlic clove
- 1/2 cup fresh basil leaves
- 1/4 cup olive oil
- 1/2 cup grated Parmigiano Reggiano
- Salt and pepper to taste

Directions:

1. Cook the fusilli in salted boiling water according to package instructions. Reserve some pasta water before draining.
2. In a food processor, combine the sun-dried tomatoes, almonds, garlic, basil, olive oil, and Parmigiano Reggiano. Blend until smooth, adding salt and pepper to taste.
3. Toss the cooked fusilli with the pesto rosso, adding reserved pasta water as needed to achieve a creamy sauce.
4. Serve with additional grated Parmigiano Reggiano.

Spaghetti with Clams (Spaghetti alle Vongole)

Ingredients:

- 400g spaghetti
- 500g fresh clams, scrubbed
- 3 tbsp olive oil
- 3 garlic cloves, thinly sliced
- 1/2 cup white wine
- 1/2 tsp red pepper flakes
- Fresh parsley, chopped
- Salt and pepper to taste
- Grated Parmigiano Reggiano (optional)

Directions:

1. Cook the spaghetti in salted boiling water according to package instructions. Reserve some pasta water before draining.
2. In a large pan, heat olive oil over medium heat. Add the garlic and cook until fragrant, about 1 minute.
3. Add the clams and white wine. Cover and cook for 5-7 minutes, until the clams open. Discard any that remain closed.
4. Add the cooked spaghetti to the pan and toss to combine. Add reserved pasta water to adjust the sauce consistency.
5. Season with red pepper flakes, salt, and pepper. Garnish with fresh parsley and serve immediately.

Lasagna Verde with Pesto

Ingredients:

- 12 sheets of lasagna noodles
- 2 cups fresh basil pesto (store-bought or homemade)
- 500g ricotta cheese
- 2 cups fresh spinach, cooked and chopped
- 2 cups mozzarella cheese, shredded
- 1/2 cup grated Parmigiano Reggiano
- Salt and pepper to taste

Directions:

1. Preheat the oven to 375°F (190°C).
2. Cook the lasagna noodles in salted boiling water according to package instructions. Drain and set aside.
3. In a mixing bowl, combine ricotta cheese, spinach, and half of the mozzarella. Season with salt and pepper.
4. In a baking dish, spread a layer of pesto on the bottom. Place a layer of lasagna noodles on top, followed by a layer of ricotta mixture and pesto. Repeat the layers, finishing with mozzarella and Parmigiano Reggiano on top.
5. Cover with foil and bake for 25 minutes. Remove the foil and bake for an additional 10 minutes to brown the top.
6. Let rest for 5 minutes before serving.

Pasta e Fagioli

Ingredients:

- 400g ditalini or small pasta
- 2 tbsp olive oil
- 1 onion, chopped
- 2 garlic cloves, minced
- 2 cans (400g each) cannellini beans, drained and rinsed
- 4 cups chicken or vegetable broth
- 1 can (400g) diced tomatoes
- 1/2 tsp dried rosemary
- Salt and pepper to taste
- Fresh parsley, chopped
- Grated Parmigiano Reggiano for serving

Directions:

1. In a large pot, heat olive oil over medium heat. Add onion and garlic and cook until softened, about 5 minutes.
2. Stir in the beans, broth, diced tomatoes, rosemary, salt, and pepper. Bring to a boil, then lower the heat and simmer for 15 minutes.
3. Add the pasta and cook until tender, about 10 minutes.
4. Serve with fresh parsley and grated Parmigiano Reggiano.

Macaroni and Cheese (Italian Style)

Ingredients:

- 400g elbow macaroni
- 2 cups whole milk
- 1 cup heavy cream
- 1 tbsp butter
- 2 tbsp flour
- 1 1/2 cups Pecorino Romano, grated
- 1/2 cup Parmigiano Reggiano, grated
- Salt and pepper to taste
- Fresh parsley, chopped (optional)

Directions:

1. Cook the macaroni in salted boiling water according to package instructions. Drain and set aside.
2. In a medium saucepan, melt butter over medium heat. Add the flour and cook for 1-2 minutes, whisking constantly.
3. Gradually add the milk and cream, whisking until the mixture thickens, about 5 minutes.
4. Stir in the grated cheeses, salt, and pepper. Toss the cooked macaroni in the sauce until well coated.
5. Serve with a sprinkle of fresh parsley.

Ravioli with Butter and Parmesan

Ingredients:

- 400g ravioli (store-bought or homemade)
- 4 tbsp unsalted butter
- 1/2 cup Parmigiano Reggiano, grated
- Fresh sage leaves (optional)
- Salt and pepper to taste

Directions:

1. Cook the ravioli in salted boiling water according to package instructions. Reserve some pasta water before draining.
2. In a large pan, melt butter over medium heat. If using sage leaves, add them to the butter and cook for 2 minutes until crispy.
3. Add the cooked ravioli to the pan, tossing gently in the butter. Add some reserved pasta water if needed to coat the ravioli.
4. Season with salt and pepper, then garnish with grated Parmigiano Reggiano. Serve immediately.

Fregola Sarda with Lobster

Ingredients:

- 400g fregola sarda (or couscous as an alternative)
- 2 lobster tails, shelled and chopped
- 2 tbsp olive oil
- 3 garlic cloves, minced
- 1/2 cup dry white wine
- 1 cup fish stock
- 1/2 tsp red pepper flakes
- Zest of 1 lemon
- Fresh parsley, chopped
- Salt and pepper to taste

Directions:

1. Cook the fregola sarda in salted boiling water according to package instructions. Drain and set aside.
2. In a large pan, heat olive oil over medium heat. Add garlic and cook for 1 minute.
3. Add lobster chunks and cook for 3-4 minutes until just cooked through. Remove and set aside.
4. In the same pan, add wine and fish stock, scraping the bottom of the pan to release any flavorful bits. Simmer for 5-7 minutes to reduce.
5. Add the fregola, red pepper flakes, lemon zest, and lobster back into the pan. Toss to combine and cook for another 2-3 minutes, adding salt and pepper to taste.
6. Garnish with fresh parsley before serving.

Tortelloni with Butternut Squash and Brown Butter

Ingredients:

- 400g tortelloni (filled with butternut squash, if available)
- 4 tbsp unsalted butter
- 1 tbsp sage leaves, chopped
- 1/4 cup grated Parmigiano Reggiano
- Salt and pepper to taste
- Fresh sage leaves for garnish (optional)

Directions:

1. Cook the tortelloni in salted boiling water according to package instructions. Drain and set aside.
2. In a large pan, melt the butter over medium heat and cook until it begins to brown and smells nutty, about 4 minutes.
3. Add chopped sage and cook for an additional minute until fragrant.
4. Toss the cooked tortelloni in the brown butter, stirring gently to coat.
5. Season with salt and pepper and sprinkle with grated Parmigiano Reggiano. Garnish with fresh sage leaves and serve.

Penne alla Vodka

Ingredients:

- 400g penne pasta
- 2 tbsp olive oil
- 1 small onion, chopped
- 3 garlic cloves, minced
- 1/2 cup vodka
- 1 can (400g) crushed tomatoes
- 1/2 cup heavy cream
- 1/2 tsp red pepper flakes
- Salt and pepper to taste
- Fresh basil, chopped
- Grated Parmigiano Reggiano for serving

Directions:

1. Cook the penne in salted boiling water according to package instructions. Drain, reserving some pasta water.
2. In a large pan, heat olive oil over medium heat. Add the onion and garlic and sauté until softened, about 5 minutes.
3. Add vodka to the pan and cook for 2-3 minutes, allowing the alcohol to evaporate.
4. Stir in the crushed tomatoes and simmer for 10 minutes.
5. Add the cream, red pepper flakes, salt, and pepper. Simmer for another 5 minutes until the sauce thickens.
6. Toss the cooked penne into the sauce, adding reserved pasta water to reach the desired consistency.
7. Garnish with fresh basil and serve with grated Parmigiano Reggiano.

Farfalle with Smoked Salmon and Cream

Ingredients:

- 400g farfalle pasta
- 200g smoked salmon, sliced into strips
- 1 tbsp olive oil
- 1 small onion, finely chopped
- 1 cup heavy cream
- 1/2 tsp lemon zest
- 1 tbsp fresh dill, chopped
- Salt and pepper to taste
- Fresh lemon wedges for serving

Directions:

1. Cook the farfalle in salted boiling water according to package instructions. Drain and set aside.
2. In a large pan, heat olive oil over medium heat. Add onion and cook until softened, about 4 minutes.
3. Stir in the heavy cream and lemon zest, cooking for another 3 minutes until the sauce begins to thicken.
4. Add the smoked salmon and cook for 2 minutes.
5. Toss the farfalle in the cream sauce, adding salt and pepper to taste.
6. Garnish with fresh dill and serve with lemon wedges.

Spaghetti with Meatballs

Ingredients:

- 400g spaghetti
- 500g ground beef
- 1 egg
- 1/2 cup breadcrumbs
- 1/4 cup grated Parmigiano Reggiano
- 1 garlic clove, minced
- 1/4 cup parsley, chopped
- Salt and pepper to taste
- 2 cups marinara sauce
- Olive oil for frying

Directions:

1. Preheat the oven to 375°F (190°C).
2. In a bowl, combine ground beef, egg, breadcrumbs, Parmigiano Reggiano, garlic, parsley, salt, and pepper. Mix until well combined and shape into meatballs.
3. Heat olive oil in a large skillet over medium heat. Fry the meatballs until browned on all sides, then transfer to a baking dish and bake for 20 minutes.
4. In the same skillet, heat marinara sauce over medium heat. Once the meatballs are done, add them to the sauce and simmer for 10 minutes.
5. Cook the spaghetti in salted boiling water according to package instructions. Drain and toss with meatballs and sauce.
6. Serve with extra Parmigiano Reggiano and fresh parsley.

Penne with Sausage and Peppers

Ingredients:

- 400g penne pasta
- 2 sausages, casing removed and crumbled
- 1 red bell pepper, sliced
- 1 green bell pepper, sliced
- 1 onion, sliced
- 3 garlic cloves, minced
- 1 can (400g) crushed tomatoes
- 1/2 tsp red pepper flakes
- Salt and pepper to taste
- Fresh basil, chopped
- Grated Parmigiano Reggiano for serving

Directions:

1. Cook the penne in salted boiling water according to package instructions. Drain and set aside.
2. In a large pan, sauté the sausage over medium heat until browned, breaking it apart with a spoon. Remove and set aside.
3. In the same pan, sauté the peppers, onion, and garlic until softened, about 5 minutes.
4. Stir in the crushed tomatoes, red pepper flakes, salt, and pepper. Simmer for 10 minutes.
5. Add the cooked sausage and penne to the sauce, tossing to combine.
6. Garnish with fresh basil and serve with grated Parmigiano Reggiano.

Capellini with Cherry Tomatoes and Basil

Ingredients:

- 400g capellini (angel hair pasta)
- 2 tbsp olive oil
- 2 cups cherry tomatoes, halved
- 2 garlic cloves, minced
- 1/2 cup fresh basil, chopped
- Salt and pepper to taste
- Grated Parmigiano Reggiano for serving

Directions:

1. Cook the capellini in salted boiling water according to package instructions. Drain, reserving some pasta water.
2. In a large pan, heat olive oil over medium heat. Add the garlic and cook for 1 minute until fragrant.
3. Add the cherry tomatoes and cook for 5 minutes until softened.
4. Add the cooked capellini and toss to combine, adding reserved pasta water if necessary.
5. Season with salt and pepper, then garnish with fresh basil and serve with grated Parmigiano Reggiano.

Gnocchi with Gorgonzola and Walnuts

Ingredients:

- 400g gnocchi
- 3 tbsp unsalted butter
- 100g Gorgonzola cheese, crumbled
- 1/4 cup walnuts, chopped
- 1/2 cup heavy cream
- Salt and pepper to taste
- Fresh parsley, chopped for garnish

Directions:

1. Cook the gnocchi in salted boiling water according to package instructions. Drain and set aside.
2. In a large pan, melt butter over medium heat. Add walnuts and cook for 2-3 minutes until toasted.
3. Stir in Gorgonzola and heavy cream, cooking until the cheese melts and the sauce becomes smooth.
4. Toss the gnocchi in the sauce, adding salt and pepper to taste.
5. Garnish with fresh parsley before serving.

Cavatelli with Sausage and Broccoli

Ingredients:

- 400g cavatelli pasta
- 2 sausages, casing removed and crumbled
- 1 bunch broccoli, cut into florets
- 3 garlic cloves, minced
- 1/2 tsp red pepper flakes
- 1/4 cup grated Parmigiano Reggiano
- Olive oil for sautéing
- Salt and pepper to taste
- Fresh parsley, chopped for garnish

Directions:

1. Cook the cavatelli in salted boiling water according to package instructions. Drain and set aside, reserving some pasta water.
2. In a large pan, heat olive oil over medium heat. Add the sausage and cook until browned, breaking it apart with a spoon.
3. Add the garlic and red pepper flakes, cooking for 1 minute.
4. In a separate pot, blanch the broccoli in boiling water for 3-4 minutes until tender. Drain and add to the sausage mixture.
5. Toss the cooked cavatelli into the pan with sausage and broccoli, adding some pasta water to help combine.
6. Season with salt and pepper, then sprinkle with grated Parmigiano Reggiano and fresh parsley. Serve warm.

Lasagna with Ricotta and Spinach

Ingredients:

- 12 lasagna noodles
- 500g ricotta cheese
- 300g spinach, cooked and drained
- 2 cups marinara sauce
- 1/2 cup grated Parmigiano Reggiano
- 1/2 cup shredded mozzarella
- 1 egg
- 2 tbsp olive oil
- Salt and pepper to taste
- Fresh basil leaves for garnish

Directions:

1. Preheat the oven to 375°F (190°C).
2. Cook the lasagna noodles according to package instructions. Drain and set aside.
3. In a bowl, combine ricotta, spinach, egg, salt, and pepper. Mix until well combined.
4. In a baking dish, spread a thin layer of marinara sauce on the bottom. Layer the lasagna noodles, followed by the ricotta-spinach mixture, and some marinara sauce. Repeat the layers, ending with a layer of sauce.
5. Sprinkle the top with grated Parmigiano Reggiano and shredded mozzarella.
6. Cover the dish with foil and bake for 25 minutes, then remove the foil and bake for an additional 10 minutes until golden and bubbly.
7. Garnish with fresh basil leaves before serving.

Pici with Garlic and Olive Oil

Ingredients:

- 400g pici pasta (or thick spaghetti)
- 4 tbsp olive oil
- 4 garlic cloves, sliced
- 1/4 tsp red pepper flakes
- 1/4 cup grated Pecorino Romano
- Salt and pepper to taste
- Fresh parsley, chopped

Directions:

1. Cook the pici in salted boiling water according to package instructions. Drain, reserving some pasta water.
2. In a large pan, heat olive oil over medium heat. Add the garlic and cook until golden brown, about 2 minutes.
3. Add red pepper flakes and toss to combine.
4. Add the cooked pici to the pan, tossing to coat in the garlic oil. Add reserved pasta water to create a silky sauce.
5. Season with salt and pepper, then sprinkle with grated Pecorino Romano and fresh parsley before serving.

Strozzapreti with Sausage and Mushrooms

Ingredients:

- 400g strozzapreti pasta
- 2 sausages, casing removed and crumbled
- 200g mushrooms, sliced
- 1 onion, chopped
- 3 garlic cloves, minced
- 1/2 cup white wine
- 2 cups marinara sauce
- 1/4 cup grated Parmigiano Reggiano
- Salt and pepper to taste
- Fresh basil for garnish

Directions:

1. Cook the strozzapreti in salted boiling water according to package instructions. Drain and set aside.
2. In a large pan, cook the sausage over medium heat until browned. Add the mushrooms and onion, cooking for 5-7 minutes until softened.
3. Add the garlic and cook for another 1 minute.
4. Pour in the white wine, scraping the pan to release any browned bits. Let it reduce for 2-3 minutes.
5. Stir in the marinara sauce and simmer for 10 minutes.
6. Toss the cooked strozzapreti into the sauce, adding salt and pepper to taste.
7. Sprinkle with grated Parmigiano Reggiano and garnish with fresh basil. Serve warm.

Fettuccine with Asparagus and Parmesan

Ingredients:

- 400g fettuccine pasta
- 1 bunch asparagus, trimmed and cut into 2-inch pieces
- 2 tbsp olive oil
- 3 garlic cloves, minced
- 1/2 cup heavy cream
- 1/4 cup grated Parmigiano Reggiano
- Salt and pepper to taste
- Fresh lemon zest for garnish

Directions:

1. Cook the fettuccine in salted boiling water according to package instructions. Drain and set aside, reserving some pasta water.
2. In a large pan, heat olive oil over medium heat. Add the asparagus and sauté for 3-4 minutes until tender.
3. Add garlic and cook for another 1 minute.
4. Stir in the heavy cream and simmer for 5 minutes.
5. Add the cooked fettuccine to the pan, tossing to coat in the sauce. Add reserved pasta water if needed to reach the desired consistency.
6. Season with salt and pepper, then sprinkle with grated Parmigiano Reggiano and fresh lemon zest before serving.

Linguine with Lobster

Ingredients:

- 400g linguine pasta
- 2 lobster tails, shelled and chopped
- 3 tbsp olive oil
- 2 garlic cloves, minced
- 1/2 cup dry white wine
- 1/2 cup heavy cream
- 1/4 tsp red pepper flakes
- Salt and pepper to taste
- Fresh parsley, chopped

Directions:

1. Cook the linguine in salted boiling water according to package instructions. Drain and set aside.
2. In a large pan, heat olive oil over medium heat. Add garlic and cook for 1 minute.
3. Add lobster chunks and cook for 3-4 minutes until just cooked through.
4. Pour in the white wine, letting it reduce for 2 minutes.
5. Stir in the heavy cream and red pepper flakes, simmering for 3-4 minutes.
6. Add the cooked linguine to the pan, tossing to combine.
7. Season with salt and pepper, then garnish with fresh parsley before serving.

Pasta al Pomodoro

Ingredients:

- 400g pasta (spaghetti, penne, or your choice)
- 4 large tomatoes, peeled and chopped
- 3 tbsp olive oil
- 3 garlic cloves, minced
- 1/4 tsp red pepper flakes
- Fresh basil, chopped
- Salt and pepper to taste
- Grated Parmigiano Reggiano for serving

Directions:

1. Cook the pasta in salted boiling water according to package instructions. Drain and set aside.
2. In a large pan, heat olive oil over medium heat. Add the garlic and cook until fragrant, about 1 minute.
3. Add the tomatoes and cook for 8-10 minutes, mashing them with a spoon as they cook.
4. Season with red pepper flakes, salt, and pepper.
5. Toss the cooked pasta in the sauce, adding a bit of pasta water if needed to help combine.
6. Garnish with fresh basil and serve with grated Parmigiano Reggiano.

Spaghetti with Zucchini and Mint

Ingredients:

- 400g spaghetti
- 2 medium zucchinis, julienned
- 2 tbsp olive oil
- 2 garlic cloves, minced
- 1/4 cup fresh mint, chopped
- Salt and pepper to taste
- Grated Parmigiano Reggiano for serving

Directions:

1. Cook the spaghetti in salted boiling water according to package instructions. Drain and set aside, reserving some pasta water.
2. In a large pan, heat olive oil over medium heat. Add garlic and cook until fragrant, about 1 minute.
3. Add the zucchini and sauté for 3-4 minutes until tender but still crisp.
4. Toss the cooked spaghetti into the pan with zucchini, adding reserved pasta water if needed to combine.
5. Season with salt and pepper, then sprinkle with fresh mint and grated Parmigiano Reggiano before serving.

Orecchiette with Sausage and Kale

Ingredients:

- 400g orecchiette pasta
- 2 sausages, casing removed and crumbled
- 1 bunch kale, chopped
- 3 garlic cloves, minced
- 1/2 tsp red pepper flakes
- 1/4 cup grated Pecorino Romano
- Olive oil for sautéing
- Salt and pepper to taste
- Fresh lemon zest for garnish

Directions:

1. Cook the orecchiette in salted boiling water according to package instructions. Drain, reserving some pasta water.
2. In a large pan, heat olive oil over medium heat. Add the sausage and cook until browned, breaking it apart with a spoon.
3. Add the garlic and red pepper flakes, cooking for 1 minute.
4. Add the kale and sauté until wilted, about 4-5 minutes.
5. Toss in the cooked orecchiette, adding some reserved pasta water to help combine.
6. Season with salt and pepper, then sprinkle with grated Pecorino Romano. Garnish with fresh lemon zest before serving.

Mafaldini with Shrimp and Saffron

Ingredients:

- 400g mafaldini pasta
- 300g shrimp, peeled and deveined
- 1/2 tsp saffron threads
- 1/2 cup dry white wine
- 1/2 cup heavy cream
- 2 garlic cloves, minced
- Olive oil for sautéing
- Salt and pepper to taste
- Fresh parsley, chopped

Directions:

1. Cook the mafaldini in salted boiling water according to package instructions. Drain, reserving some pasta water.
2. In a small bowl, steep the saffron threads in warm water for about 5 minutes.
3. In a large pan, heat olive oil over medium heat. Add the shrimp and cook for 2-3 minutes until pink. Remove and set aside.
4. Add garlic to the same pan and cook for 1 minute.
5. Pour in the white wine, scraping the pan to release any browned bits. Add the saffron with its water and let it simmer for 3 minutes.
6. Stir in the heavy cream and cook for another 3 minutes until the sauce thickens slightly.
7. Add the cooked mafaldini and shrimp to the pan, tossing to combine.
8. Season with salt and pepper, then garnish with fresh parsley before serving.

Lasagna Caprese

Ingredients:

- 12 lasagna noodles
- 300g fresh mozzarella, sliced
- 2 cups cherry tomatoes, halved
- 1/4 cup fresh basil, chopped
- 2 cups marinara sauce
- 1/4 cup grated Parmigiano Reggiano
- Olive oil for drizzling
- Salt and pepper to taste

Directions:

1. Preheat the oven to 375°F (190°C).
2. Cook the lasagna noodles according to package instructions. Drain and set aside.
3. In a baking dish, spread a thin layer of marinara sauce on the bottom. Layer the lasagna noodles, followed by mozzarella, tomatoes, basil, and more marinara sauce. Repeat layers, ending with mozzarella and sauce.
4. Drizzle with olive oil and sprinkle with grated Parmigiano Reggiano.
5. Cover the dish with foil and bake for 25 minutes. Remove foil and bake for another 10 minutes until bubbly and golden.
6. Garnish with fresh basil leaves before serving.

Pasta alla Caprese

Ingredients:

- 400g pasta (spaghetti, penne, or your choice)
- 300g cherry tomatoes, halved
- 1/4 cup fresh mozzarella, torn into pieces
- 1/4 cup fresh basil, chopped
- 2 tbsp olive oil
- 1 tbsp balsamic vinegar
- Salt and pepper to taste

Directions:

1. Cook the pasta in salted boiling water according to package instructions. Drain, reserving some pasta water.
2. In a large pan, heat olive oil over medium heat. Add the cherry tomatoes and cook for 2-3 minutes until softened.
3. Stir in balsamic vinegar, then toss in the cooked pasta.
4. Add mozzarella, basil, and some reserved pasta water to help combine.
5. Season with salt and pepper, then serve with extra basil for garnish.

Penne with Roasted Vegetables

Ingredients:

- 400g penne pasta
- 1 zucchini, sliced
- 1 red bell pepper, chopped
- 1 eggplant, cubed
- 2 tbsp olive oil
- 3 garlic cloves, minced
- 1/2 tsp dried oregano
- 1/4 cup grated Parmigiano Reggiano
- Salt and pepper to taste

Directions:

1. Preheat the oven to 400°F (200°C).
2. Toss the zucchini, bell pepper, and eggplant with olive oil, salt, pepper, and oregano. Roast in the oven for 20-25 minutes, or until tender.
3. Meanwhile, cook the penne in salted boiling water according to package instructions. Drain, reserving some pasta water.
4. In a large pan, heat olive oil over medium heat. Add garlic and cook for 1 minute.
5. Toss the roasted vegetables and cooked pasta into the pan, adding some reserved pasta water to combine.
6. Sprinkle with Parmigiano Reggiano and serve.

Ravioli with Sweet Potato and Sage

Ingredients:

- 400g ravioli with sweet potato filling
- 2 tbsp butter
- 10 fresh sage leaves
- 1/4 cup grated Parmigiano Reggiano
- Salt and pepper to taste

Directions:

1. Cook the ravioli in salted boiling water according to package instructions. Drain and set aside.
2. In a large pan, melt butter over medium heat. Add the sage leaves and cook for 1-2 minutes until crispy.
3. Toss the cooked ravioli in the sage butter, seasoning with salt and pepper.
4. Sprinkle with grated Parmigiano Reggiano before serving.

Fettuccine with Spicy Sausage

Ingredients:

- 400g fettuccine pasta
- 2 spicy sausages, casing removed and crumbled
- 1 onion, chopped
- 2 garlic cloves, minced
- 1/2 cup dry white wine
- 2 cups heavy cream
- 1/4 cup grated Pecorino Romano
- Salt and pepper to taste

Directions:

1. Cook the fettuccine in salted boiling water according to package instructions. Drain and set aside.
2. In a large pan, cook the sausage over medium heat until browned. Add the onion and garlic, cooking for 5 minutes until softened.
3. Pour in the white wine and let it reduce for 2-3 minutes.
4. Stir in the heavy cream and simmer for 5 minutes.
5. Add the cooked fettuccine to the pan and toss to combine.
6. Season with salt and pepper, then sprinkle with grated Pecorino Romano before serving.

Rigatoni with Eggplant and Ricotta

Ingredients:

- 400g rigatoni pasta
- 1 large eggplant, cubed
- 2 tbsp olive oil
- 2 garlic cloves, minced
- 1/4 cup fresh ricotta
- 1/4 cup grated Parmigiano Reggiano
- Salt and pepper to taste
- Fresh basil leaves for garnish

Directions:

1. Cook the rigatoni in salted boiling water according to package instructions. Drain and set aside.
2. In a large pan, heat olive oil over medium heat. Add the eggplant and cook for 8-10 minutes, stirring occasionally, until softened and browned.
3. Add garlic and cook for 1 minute.
4. Toss in the cooked rigatoni, adding some pasta water to help combine.
5. Stir in the ricotta, then season with salt and pepper.
6. Sprinkle with grated Parmigiano Reggiano and garnish with fresh basil before serving.

Pappardelle with Duck Ragù

Ingredients:

- 400g pappardelle pasta
- 2 duck legs, cooked and shredded
- 1 onion, chopped
- 2 garlic cloves, minced
- 1/2 cup red wine
- 2 cups tomato sauce
- 1/4 tsp dried thyme
- Salt and pepper to taste
- Fresh parsley for garnish

Directions:

1. Cook the pappardelle in salted boiling water according to package instructions. Drain and set aside.
2. In a large pan, sauté the onion and garlic in olive oil over medium heat for 5 minutes.
3. Add the shredded duck and cook for 3-4 minutes.
4. Pour in the red wine, scraping the pan to release any browned bits. Let the wine reduce for 3 minutes.
5. Stir in the tomato sauce and thyme. Simmer for 15 minutes.
6. Toss the cooked pappardelle in the duck ragù, then season with salt and pepper.
7. Garnish with fresh parsley before serving.